Pieces of my Pieces: Uncensored

By: Jason Dommell

Cover designed by: Jason Dommell

Edited by Dr. William Martin

ISBN 978-1-257-62494-2 90000

9 781257 624942

Thank you
to all of my friends and family that have encouraged my writing
especially my parents Bob and Sue,
I love you

Thank you
to those who have influenced my writing
without you none of this would have been possible.

Thank you
to Dr. William Martin
whose knowledge, and expertise helped shape this book
into what it is today.

Table of Contents

Preface

I am writing the preface to my book for a couple of reasons; to let the reader know my exact reasoning for writing the book, and to remind myself the same. This is my first trial into the writing arena; I know that it will never get completed in one day and if I don't get it on paper now, I may never.

I started writing poetry when I was a senior in high school, although it was not good by any means; it was a place to start, learn and to grow from. In the early stages I found myself rhyming a lot. This style challenged me because I had to come up with new and interesting ways to say what I wanted to say. It wasn't until I abandoned the rhyme scheme that I really began to grow. Using a freestyle form of writing my poetry was so much more freeing. I was able to better express myself on paper and as I moved up this steppingstone I chose specific words within my writing, not for rhyming purposes, but for double meanings and interesting ambiguity. I use the word 'stepping stone' because even my early freestyle isn't fabulous.

Directly out of high school, I became involved with and later married my childhood friend and neighbor. At the age of eighteen she gave birth to a son, and I dove head first and blind into the idea of having a family. My marriage took my writing in an entirely new direction, and because a writer generally writes about what he knows, I write a lot on my family, particularly my wife and the marriage itself.

Just recently I toyed with the idea of publishing my poetry, so I sent fifty or so random poems (the majority regarding my marriage as I believe they are the strongest) to a friend of mine who was writing a book regarding her own life at the time. Her publisher returned my poetry claiming that I had nothing more than a 'book of hate'. He wanted me to reexamine my poetry and write 'how these negative experiences make me into a better person'. For the longest time, I refused to go down that road, but with age comes wisdom, and with wisdom, a sense of clarity.

My moment of clarity came when my seventeen-year-old sister-in-law came to my house with a novel made up of chronological poetry. I must admit that I never did read it, but the idea of writing a novel by means of poetry set in chronological order inspired me to re-look at my 'book of hate'. I gathered up every poem that I had ever written about my relationship with my wife before, during and after my marriage and set them in chronological order. (Thank God I date everything.) What I saw astounded me, there was not only a growth in my writing, but when put together, they map the rise and fall of my marriage.

It is my hopes that by including all of the poems together in the order that they were written. The 'book of hate' will take on a new life and a new beginning.

With that, I dedicate this book, to my friend, without her guidance these individual writings would still be nothing but a 'book of hate', but together they are….

Pieces of my Pieces

WARNING
THE MATERIAL IN THIS EDITION CONTAINS ADULT THEMES AND ARE SEXUAL IN NATURE.

Chapter One: ***This Skin***

Before exploring my marriage and inevitably my wife, I feel that it is important to bring my own skeletons out of the closet first. This is being done for three reasons; one, my wife is embarrassed and mad that I would ever dream of publishing my poetry, indeed airing our 'dirty laundry' and most personal, intimate moments; two, I am a part of this marriage and therefore to better understand it, both sides must be looked at, scrutinized and taken apart in order for it to be put back together correctly later; and three, the first poem in this collection is the first poem that I ever wrote where I was able to successfully convey on paper how I truly felt. Growing up with Cerebral Palsy (however slight) was not, and in some cases still today at the age of thirty, easy.

Walking Tall

I pray that someday I can walk
Free of the chains that God put on my legs.
That one-day,
I can walk with my
Head held high, my back straight, and my heels
Buried deep within the dust.

When I walk down the hall,
All eyes turn to me.
Conversations stop and the silence thickens.
Nothing can be heard except for the clack of my crooked footsteps.
So, when walking down the hall,
I close my eyes and listen to my own voice,
Rather than the mocking whispers. 9-3-97

Walking Blind

I walk as normal as I know how, heel-toe
Heal-toe. I hear
My grandfather's voice constantly reminding me to stay away
From my usual flat steps.
He watches me walk, everybody does.
He pretends not to notice how crooked
My steps are. He smiles, telling me how good I walk
When I try.
His lies are simple, but I know he loves me,
And I love him. At least someone makes me feel normal.
Even the mirror frowns.
Heal-toe.
I try to remember, to concentrate on each precious step,
But it's not easy.
I've walked a lot of miles and I'm not even half way home.
I'm tired of being seen for what I have.
It may be physical, but it's not a disability.
People just refuse to learn that.
They'd rather stare
They'd rather laugh
They'd rather imitate.
I can't keep my eyes closed forever.
I don't like the dark. 11-7-97

Someone Else's Shoes

I ran from her,
Racing down the hall as she screamed after me.
Her words echoed off the walls, pounded in my ears.
I stopped.
I couldn't run form her cruel remarks, and
I couldn't deny that it wasn't the first time.
Called on a technicality, I can't change it now.
I wish that I could be like everybody else.
  To walk into a room and not watch everybody's eyes follow my footsteps,
  Tracing my crooked path with their own perfect feet.
  To walk down the hall and not hear people crucify my body.
  Sometimes I wish that I could nail my feet to the floor.
  Maybe then people would pay attention to the rest of me.
But I'd be sacrificing a piece of me that sets me apart.
Maybe too far apart.
Some days are good, some days
I feel as though I'm running naked against traffic
Exposed to everybody.
They see my hidden scars and know how to make me bleed.
I keep forgetting to remember; I'm too busy trying to forget.
  I'm tired of my legs.
  My legs are always tired.
  I'm sick of running.
  Maybe next time I'll sit down. 11-7-97

In This Body

Live in this body
And see if you can make it a home.
The skin wrapped around my bent frame.
The shoes I wear--too tight, too loose,
Never perfect, never normal.
The label that I wear can't peel off
And won't expire.
I'd like to walk without concentrating,
Without worrying who's watching.

Live in this body
And see if your heart is as strong.
Or would you crumble
Beneath these tired legs.
Things are never easy in this flesh,
So full of scars.
I can never escape those who hurt me,
Nor the fears that grip my weary shadow,
Making it wish that it were somebody else's.

Live in this body
And see if you can keep your eyes open.
Shutting them never helps,
There's no comfort in the dark.
Maybe I will finally take a step in the right direction.
No matter which way that I choose
It's never the right one.
But I can't stand still,
And backwards is even harder. 10-10-9

Skin

The word and all of it synonyms cut
Through me, easily, every time.
I can't outrun it, I can't escape it,
It's stereotype has left a stench on my
Skin.
How do I prove that I am what I seem not to be--
Its very antonym.
I could scream it, but deaf ears can be cruel,
And sign language doesn't always work.
I've learned not to run, that only draws
More attention.
I see how fake their smiles can be, the closer they get,
Like glass
Cutting through their gums.
How they love to spit their shards
Of teeth in my face. 1-6-03

Quiet

How I hate the quiet whispers
Hidden underneath your tongue,
Concealed behind your teeth.
How I want to punch them out.
How I hate the quiet whispers,
The loudest to me, like nails
On a chalkboard shrieking down
My spine.
Do you not think that I see your eyes
Tilted up at me, burning
Through my skin?
I'm a lot tougher than I look,
On the outside.
The giggle that follows,
Ripples through the air, washes
Over me in waves of sarcasm.
I finally learned how to swim.

I hate the quiet whispers.
How I would love to yell back. 11-12-03

This Skin

This mask that I am wearing is getting old.
Like a cheap window-cling, it's starting to fold at the edges.
This skin is decaying from underneath my feet.
I keep waiting for the dust to settle but all that I do is kick
More into the air, keeping me blind.
My mind is dizzy with misinformation.
I just want to close my eyes for once,
Tightly.
I'm tired of running in every direction
At once,
But catch up is the only game that I know
How to play.
I never seem to get anywhere, as if my shoelaces
Are tied together. I keep falling,
Each time harder than the last.
I'm exhausted from walking in these shoes.
I've gone so many miles already and I'm still
Half way in the wrong direction.
I've worn out the soul
Treading this jagged path. After all this time,
I'd like to think that I've become immune to these
Sticks and stones.
But scars don't lie, no matter how big I smile.
I don't want to be me anymore, or perhaps
I am exactly what I'm looking for.
The real me, behind this mask, somewhere
Underneath this skin. Walking somewhere
Barefoot. 10-10-04

Chapter Two: ***Nobody but Me***

This is the first chapter in regards to my relationship with my wife. We were fresh out of high school, young and stupid, I was a virgin, she had just given birth to a son and was now living with her father across the street from my family and me. (Her parents are divorced.) She was looking for a way out, and I was looking for love; I found it in her son.

The poetry is not earth shattering, but it is essential to explore my changing view on love and later marriage.

A Long Little Something

It didn't happen, we paved a way through nature's course
And stopped.
Time cut our journey short. We stared, speechless
Into each other's eyes.
Even though we were together, this wall of emotions,
My emotions,
Keeps us apart. I know what journey we're on,
But in a lot of ways I'm afraid to move forward.
I don't want to go back, I don't want to stay where we are,
I want to move forward,
With you.
I find myself frozen with fear and uncertainty.
I've never traveled this road before; I don't know what lies ahead.
I do know that I want you with me,
I need you with me.
Here, we stand frozen and we won't move until I
Find the courage and the time to make that
First step.
It may come easy, it may come hard, but I need you here
Beside me, to help me through nature's course,
Until we finally reach our destination.
I don't know everything. I'm not a perfect man, but I do know that
I love you
With all of my heart, body and soul.
When I find the courage to say those words,
We can proceed.
Until then, nature will have to wait.
I hope that you can.

You hold my heart in your hands now.
What you do with it is your choice. 5-5-97

Standing Alone

I stand before you naked,
Emotionally stripped of any words.
My feelings lay like a pile of wrinkled clothes at your feet.
I'm very vulnerable as I stand and now I've
Bared all.
I'm hoping that you'll do the same. 5-8-97

Standing Still

There are many times when I feel that we've made
Giant steps in the direction we both want to go,
But then I realize that we've only made baby steps.
We may not be as close as we thought,
But at least we're not standing still. 6-2-97

A (Not so) Simple Kiss

We travel together by day, my love and I
Heart and heart, hand in hand. We are each
Half of the other. Together we make one
Body, heart, soul and love.
A love that is strong and true, that neither of us can live without.
By night, we two part our ways, first
We stare into each other's eyes, then nothing.
After, she watches me walk away,
And we both dream of that not so
Simple kiss, and wonder when and if it will
Ever happen. 6-12-97

Maybe Then

Open yourself wide and let me inside.
As I work myself deeper maybe then
I can touch your heart
The way that you've touched mine. 6-29-97

My Own

I've wanted to tell you that I love you a thousand times,
But each time I've reconsidered.
I'd rather bask in the glory of an imaginary love,
Instead of finding out that the only love felt between us
Is my own.

6-30-97

Simple Kiss

Just thinking of you and how much I'd like to do
All of the things that run though my head.
How much I'd like to touch you, kiss you, but when we're
Together nothing happens.
No matter how much that I want us to proceed, we just stand still,
I stand still,
Afraid of what a simple kiss might turn into.
I want all of the rest of it, everything.
Hopefully soon,
I'll break free of the fear that has a hold over me, and go with you
Into the future. 6-30-97

Nobody but Me

What keeps my lips from yours?
Nothing.
What keeps our bodies from becoming one?
Nobody.
Yet when we're together we seem to be separated
By sheet of glass.
We both think about it, dream about it, want it.
I know you would if I would.
What's wrong with me?
I can't wait for the future but the future won't happen,
If I don't stop living in the past.
I need your help but I'm afraid to ask.
I'm afraid where you'll take me.
My fear of the unknown is great. It keeps my feet
Securely planted on familiar territory.
I can't fly with you to unforeseeable pleasures yet.
I don't like heights, I don't want to fall.
Hopefully soon
I'll escape this childish fear that nobody but me trapped me in. 8-29-97

Chapter Three: ***Just a Dream***

Within this particular chapter, my wife and I live together and marry, we finally become intimate, I learn about her sexually history and her demons; and I bought every bit of it, hook, line and sinker. How naive I was.

*****WARNING*****

THE MATERIAL IN THE CHAPTERS THAT FOLLOW CONTAIN ADULT THEMES AND ARE SEXUAL IN NATURE.

Eventually

How does one mend a heart broken in too many pieces?
End nightmares when the dreams refuse to come?
All that I want is to heal what's inside. I don't know
If I can go deep enough.
I wish that I could penetrate more than her skin,
Flesh only goes so far.
Her body is a prisoner of her mind.
A body can heal, but a mind lies raped forever.
She died that night.
I hope that I'm strong enough to resurrect her,
To spark the feelings of lust that he took from her,
To teach her love instead of fear.
Someday I'll find a way to help her lose control
Of the urges that he has destroyed.
Maybe then she won't be afraid of the dark.
Maybe then she'll enjoy my touch and beg for more.
I can only wait while she fights her demons, and hope
That she is able to beat them.
After that, we'll truly be one,
With no top and no bottom,
Only joined
Somewhere in the middle. 10-14-98

Torn

She's torn between two women--
The one she is and the one that she wants to be--
Still baring scares that she pretends are not there.
She walks around with the biggest smile that she can fake.
Her mind keeps her trapped in a past she tried so hard to escape.
She's been mind-fucked by those who've gotten close, and
Holds on tightly to a heart raped three times over by those
Who've managed to get in.
She wonders at night if she's got enough love left to make a relationship last;
As if she truly knows what love is anymore.
She tells her secrets to a burning cigarette
Hoping the nicotine will last,
She's blaming the tears on the smoke in her eyes,
Assuring me that everything is ok.
Her past has her by the throat and she's unwilling to scream.
Afraid to let anyone in, too scared to let anything out.
Everything stays where she puts it and grows like a weed,
Consuming all that she is, until there's nothing left
But bitterness,
Leaving her cold and angry with God
For not protecting her when she had her virginity violated
At the age of fifteen,
For not helping her a year later when violence penetrated more
Then her body,
And for not saving her the birth of a son when it happened
Again;
A daily reminder that life can be cruel to someone so young.
The woman of flesh and blood, love and lust, is buried
Somewhere
Beneath the scars that still continue to bleed old blood.
She holds on to her pain and lets it control her,
Too nervous to let everything fall to the floor and just sleep
Naked for once. 10-19-98

Middle Ground

I'm out of my mind to be in this deep.
Can't go back, it's already begun.
Won't pull out, it would be over before I'm free
It's impossible to be gentle, too easy to be rough.
I can be smothering when I show too much affection,
Too insensitive when I show too little.
There is no middle ground with a woman who refuses to bend.
All that I want is to please her.
Maybe I try too hard, maybe
I don't try hard enough.
I end up breaking new promises while taping the old ones
Back together.
I long to give physical pleasure to the woman that I love, and
Only dream of receiving it back. 11-14-98

Frozen

It's not her skin that I can't touch,
Fore my hands know her body very well,
It's her heart.
I've penetrated her soft flesh many times.
It's never deep enough, never long enough.
She keeps her heart buried in a place that doesn't allow feeling.
That won't allow love.
If she can't feel it, she can't show it.
If she can't show it, she won't get hurt.
'Just lie there,' she says, 'let him satisfy himself'.
How pleasurable can love, and sex, be, with no physical affection
In return.
Even the words I love you don't work anymore,
Unless she says them first.
Hasn't happened yet.
She thinks that I'm going to break her heart,
When all that I want is to hold it.
She thinks that I'm going to rape her body,
When all that I want is to pleasure it.
I've made all the right moves. I've gone as far as I can.
It's time to get her back off of the mattress, take control of the night,
And see where her heart can take us.
I can't do it alone,
Not anymore. 3-14-99

About Last Night

We were alone
In the dark, touching. Feeling
The temperature in the room rise.
As our bodies slowly melted into one,
She said no.
Why did I start? Why
Was I allowed to take it this far?
Why did I let it bother me?
This wasn't the first time,
It won't be the last.
So I stole one last kiss,
An withdrew my body
From hers. 3-14-99

Crucified

She doesn't know how hard it is to see something so beautiful
And not be able to touch it.
She loves to tease me, exposing her body pieces at a time.
It gives her pleasure to see my body react to her every move.
As I approach her, one thing is on our minds.
We touch, we kiss, we explore, the moment is upon us
But as we reach the bed to end this foreplay
Everything stops; she goes cold, her lips run dry, no
Instead of yes.
We never get beyond this point anymore.
She's scared
That I am going to hurt her;
She's not willing to trust yet. She can't risk being raped
Again.
So, we don't make love, just a lot of foreplay.
Never more, never less.
I won't force her to do anything that she is not ready for.
I've learned to keep my feelings under control and my hands to myself.
Now-a-day's I look and don't touch.
Because I love her I won't put her through another compromising position.
When's she's ready, she'll make a move. Until then,
I'm paying for the crime of another man.
His body was rough; mine can never be gentle enough.
I don't know what she feels when she relives that rape, and she
Has no clue what it feels like to be rejected every time,
Pushed away, yelled at for wanting to show her physically
How much that I love her, denied countless kisses.
Her face is protected by her hair.
I know that I will never stop loving her.
I've crossed my heart more times than she's crossed
Her legs.
She's already been crucified.
Now it's her turn to pound in a few nails. 3-26-99

Tied Down

Will love love me back
Before my heart grows cold
Will our bodies become one
Before she pushes me away?
All that I want is to touch her.
But her hair is long and tangled.
I want to live the fairytale; my reality is just too cold.
I can't get anything but sleep with the one that my heart has chosen.
I'm waiting for her to make a move.
I'm afraid I'll wait forever. 4-22-99

Just a Dream

I fell in love with a fantasy. I thought that we could live together
Like a fairytale, so I gave up on reality
To chase a dream.
I'm wide-awake now, sleeping alone.
Love has no meaning here. Hearts are made
To be broken.
She found comfort once, in my arms
Now she pushes me away
Just far enough to give her freedom,
Close enough to ensure safety.
She retreats anytime I advance.
Love with her is a war, fought on a battlefield
That I don't feel like being on anymore. 5-27-99

Forbidden Love

You push instead of pull, keeping me at arms length.
Close enough to love you, far enough so that I can't smother you.
Your heart forgot how to love, and you're unwilling to learn again.
You're afraid that my mask will fall off,
Exposing a face that looks like the one you're trying to forget.
Making love is not an option;
You lie there avoiding my eyes,
In fear that they won't be mine.
Every night, no matter what I do, he rapes you,
Over and over again. His shadow is mine.
Your body is his, every time, until you're strong enough to give it to me.
You should've opened your heart to me, before you
Opened your legs. 9-25-99

Dear God

I fucked up.
I found out that my heart isn't as big as I thought it was.
I talk too much, to too many.
My tongue should've been cut off a long time ago.
My mouth won't stay closed. I talked her right out of my life.
I fucked up.
My life refuses to stay. Without her I'm empty, dead
To the world. I'd be nothing but a shadow,
A hallow heart buried in a watery grave, filled
With my own tears.
I had perfection in my hands, love in my grasp.
We were about to walk down the isle towards eternity
Until I tripped over my tongue. 9-25-99

Not So Gentle

I want my life back. I lost it piece by piece,
And the only thing that will make me whole again is
Time is wearing thin and so is my money.
I don't know if I'll ever be whole again.
Too many pieces of my life have been
Broken and re-broken.
I don't think that I have enough glue, and tape doesn't stick.
My life is in the hands of another woman,
My other half. Her hands are not so gentle.
Her nails are long and she likes to scratch.
I gave her everything that I had, everything that she's ever wanted,
And I'm still waiting for something in return. 10-3-99

Locked Away

Why can't you say that you love me
Before I say it first?
Why can't you tell me
Your inter-most desires or experiences,
The passion you long for.
I know these feelings exist. Somewhere
Deep inside your cold skin
Lies a fire that I just can't touch.
You keep it hidden, afraid to let go.
Afraid to be free for once.
Only once.
Your mind is locked away,
Until I find the key. 11-3-99

One

With this ring, my heart is yours.
Hold it tight, don't squeeze
Too hard, too much.
Carry it with you even in death.
So we can exist together beyond this skin.

With these vows our bodies become one.
Be gentle when you play rough.
Hard kisses in the most tender places.
Curious hands in unfamiliar territory.
Bury our tongues deep within the others throat
To ensure that secrets stay between we two.

With each kiss our love grows deeper.
Our souls let go of any emptiness
As we hold each other close,
Until we are finally whole,
Each completing what the other was lacking.

With this ring my life is yours
Everyday of every year.
I will sacrifice and I will bleed.
Anything for you,
The woman that I love. 12-20-99

Night After Night

Always tired, she is tired of living.
Life as a victim isn't sweet,
But she finds safety in it still.
Putting her head down,
Shielding her face with her hair,
She closes her eyes to calm her fears.
But it's not fear that she's escaping, it's love.
Three years have passed, and her heart has finally found comfort
In another man's arms.
She says that she wants to change, to feel love, to make love.
But she lies there, night after night dreading the dark,
Her eyes swell up
And she cries every time I come
To an end.
Afterwards, we kiss as she pulls the covers
Over her like amour, protecting her naked skin.
She prays to God to help her get better, to enjoy my gentle rhythm.
She's not strong enough yet.
So she keeps her hands and lips to herself. She prays for a miracle
But it won't happen.
Not until she wants it bad enough.
The next time we make love she hopes to join my rhythm,
But she knows she'll be flat on her back, gritting her teeth,
Waiting for the precise moment that she can open her eyes
And wipe away the tears. 12-27-99

While She Slept

In the dark, while she slept,
I ran my hands over her naked skin.
She moaned and opened herself up to me.
As my hands worked their way into her dreams,
The closer our bodies became. Our juices flowed faster,
Until they exploded from within us,
Out into the night air. It soaked our naked bodies, smeared
The newly cleaned sheets until the smell of sex was stronger
Than the Downey our bed was bathed in.
On my chest she lay close enough for my tongue
To taste. Her lips hugged my mouth as I swallowed. 1-12-00

As She Laid There

Wrist pinned to the mattress, starring at me,
As if she expected me to hold her down and rape her like
He did.
Kissing her thighs gently, she laid there cold and ridged,
Never open
To the possibility of something between the sheets.
Circles didn't do anything but make her dizzy.
My mouth went from one sweet spot to the next ascending
To her belly-button, then to her breast and when
Our eyes finally met, she looked at me as if I wasn't there and
Love wasn't being made.
She started to shake as my hands slid under her arm, until we lay
Fingertip to fingertip.
My breath in her ear, teeth on her lobe, sucking
On her neck, pushing all of the right buttons,
Too hard too fast.
She closed her eyes and swallowed.
Her whole body turned to stone, held down by the weight of
A memory.
His skin, breath, words, sweat, erection.
The moment of betrayal penetrated her defenses and she
Cried out as he rapped her mind again.
He and I are one now, joined only by gender.
I tried to comfort her, but his memory is strong, holding tight, even after four years.
Her face twisted in anguish, random tears ran
Hand-in-hand with scattered cries for help. Everything
That is mine now belongs to him.
She begged for me to stop, unaware that I was the only one who could've saved her.
She told me who I became, where she was, I could do nothing but whisper
Countless 'I love you's'
While I reminded her what my name was. I was careful
Not to get too close, she's been tricked by shadows before. 3-13-00

All About You

I need to stop running in circles before I fall.
I need to walk and look where I'm going.
I need to open my eyes; I've been in the dark for far too long,
But I'm afraid of what I'll see.
I've gotten to where I am as fast as I could,
Now, I don't know if this is where I want to be.
I need to make a choice, but I don't want to.

I want to take back control, but I don't know where I lost it.
I want to know what fifty-fifty feels like,
I'm tired of ninety-ten.
I want to say I love you and hear it back,
And have her mean it this time.
I want my wife back, I already have a mother. 12-5-02

And Me

I could tell you that I love you
But nothing gets through the armor that you've built
Around your soft skin.
I could show you how cold you've become,
But I'd have to throw you in the fire and
I don't know if I have the heart to watch you burn.
Maybe I should.
Things used to be different, we used to be different.
What happened to 'us'?
All that I see now is 'you' and 'I'.
How did we get to where we are?
How do we get back before you forget
How to smile and I, how to laugh.
Before loving each other becomes impossible and
Our marriage a mystery.

How do we fix what is broken when we don't even
Know when it cracked? 11-25-03

Chapter Four: ***Matters of the Heart***

The writing within these set of pages is very dark, yet I feel that it is my best. I explored more with the words and language that I chose to use and dabbled with a little religion.

Darkness

If we are truly opposite then I am the light and she, the dark
My children are scared of the dark it has everything to hide.
Her blackness is endless almost impenetrable, cold and empty.
I cannot leave for I am the light, once a bright light.
She is powerful and I am fading.
She would swallow them whole
If I left.
I used to illuminate my whole world, now I only seem to shine
In the hole that is left.
The only thing that I am good at any more is helping cast shadows,
Soon I'll do nothing but glow in the dark.
Even then, she'll chase away any spark that I have left until I am nothing
But a smoldering pile of ashes.
Like a dark cloud she looms over my head.
Raining on any ray of light that might shine through.
She brings her thunder and lightning
Leaving no chance for rainbows, only puddles that pool
And ripple into steams of tears.
My children can't swim. They will drown without me
Helping them float.
I am the light, I cannot leave.
She digs at me until I am hollower than she is,
Yet my smile prevails, even though my teeth are cracked.
My patience has worn thin after eight years, but
I'm hanging on by a fool's hope that tomorrow's storm will be less
Than today's.
I pray for a break, so that I may have just a moment
To shine.
After all, I am the light.
Darkness would simply be nothingness without
The light.
Yet, I feel like nothingness in the dark
I cannot leave.
I cannot leave.
Not yet
Not now. 5-2-04

Just Evil

An angel was she,
I saw Heaven in her eyes, God
In her womb.
How much I wanted to experience her grace.
How blind I was.
She crucified me after forty days.
She loves to pound in her rusty nails,
Never in the same place twice.
She has molted her wings
And traded them in for thirty gold pieces.
Love no longer grows in our garden.
Where was that damn tree before I willingly
Accepted my ring of thorns?
I've tasted her forbidden fruit, Oh, the sweet taste of poison.
Why did I have to swallow?
Yet I stayed.
Where would I go if,
When I leave.
My spirit has been resurrected three times.
They're too young to fly on their own.
And I'm not ready for the desert.
I've carried this silent weight for years, and have
Fallen more times than I'd like to admit.
I've become numb to her endless lashes.
Being pussy whipped hurts, yet
There is pleasure in pain, for both of us.

An angel was she,
Never, once did I see her forked tongue.
Or maybe I just liked how it felt to be kissed.
Affection is an oasis, that's all
She is, an illusion in the desert, brought on
By a thirst for love.
I have been bitten hard, and I acknowledge my pain,
Yet, I stay.
It is a long, lonely journey though the sand and
I'm not ready to find myself.
She has denied me more than three times
Yet I stay
Yet I stay
Yet I stay, Fore an angel am I.

5-5-0

Precious Pain

There was a firmness in her lips that I haven't felt
In a long time,
As we lay there kissing in the dark, this kind of love
Is a rarity and time becomes precious.
The moon casts shadows that I've envisioned many times,
In my minds eye.
Touch is a luxury, this night, one that I can rarely afford,
But I save my pennies, when I can, for she spends
Everything else. 7-27-04

Never Enough

I'm getting tired of my life being
Upside-down.
Her emotions have become flat, and mine
Unpredictable.
She only seems to have two anymore:
Anger and hate,
Both wrongly directed at the man trying the hardest to
Love her.
My marriage is inside out, my seams are showing,
What's left of them.
Eight years, and she's managed to strip me,
In more ways than one,
Of my own emotions, until I am as barren
As she is.
We don't talk anymore, spending more time apart.
The beginning of the end happened a long time ago and
We both refuse to acknowledge when and where.
I do love her, when she smiles, laughs, touches me, draws me into her.
She's stopped doing those things.
But I still love her, somewhere underneath it all
For that reason, I cannot leave her,
As much as I want to.
My children remind me of the love that was made,
Once upon a time.
We seem to never get passed snuggling anymore.
Sex, to her, in unimportant, a marriage
Can survive without it. Yet
Our marriage is withering around us.
On the rare occasions that love is made, she always receives,
Never gives.   Never.
My heart tries very hard to love her, but my body is
Lonely.
I want to be on the receiving end. For a change.
It gets harder every day, to love someone who doesn't
Love back.   7-27-04

Pieces of my Pieces

I loved the little girl that nobody loved.
She wanted too much and more,
and I gave it to her.
Now, eight years later, I have no more love to give.
I feel hollowed out as empty and jagged as she is.
She has stripped me of everything that I called my own.
I don't remember what it's like to be me anymore.
I've been whittled away to her perception of me.
I can't figure out when and where I went wrong.
Did I fall apart or did she break me to pieces?
That's all she loves anyway, just my pieces.
Pieces of my pieces.
That way, she never commits herself one hundred percent.
All that I ever asked for was fifty percent, I'm lucky
If I get twenty.
She taunts me at an arms length.
Close enough to touch her, but far enough away where
I can't feel her.
She allows me to see how beautiful her body can be
When not covered up by all of her negative emotions,
But very rarely, do I get to experience her beauty.
(Only in a dream, or if she falls asleep first).
Love bares a high cost, and right now I'm willing to pay.
I always wonder what will shatter first
Our splintering marriage, our fragmented love,
ME.
Or maybe I'll finally get lucky, and she, with her
Crazy-glued façade, will crumble,
Exposing the real her to the world.
For the first time, for the last time.
It would be nice to watch her bleed for a change. 10-4-04

Still Now

I fell in love when my heart was still new and I didn't know
What love looked like.
For me, her beauty alone called to me.
The warmth of her skin awakened my heart and I gave it to her.
If I could've penetrated her heart, then I would have felt
How cold and empty it was, is
Still now.
Eight years later, her beauty is cliché to me.
Skin deep.
How shallow she can be.
She saw stability and security in my blind eyes, so she
Gave herself to me.   Halfheartedly.
Like a fool, I took it, not realizing how many pieces that her heart was in.

Still now,
I'm finding missing pieces.
Love is hard work when you're carrying both sides.
For her, I was a much-needed shelter.
Matches in hand, she's waiting for the day that she can
Burn me down.
At least I'd finally get a spark out of her.   11-9-04

Now and Never

I've sacrificed more that I'm willing to admit to. For what?
A love that I've never received?
Eight years have passed and her promise of change still lies
Unfulfilled.
A heart I've never held?
It's crumbled every time that I've tried.
A body I've never touched?
At least while she's awake. Thankfully, she sleeps like an angel,
My little devil does.
Only then, does she loosen her tail from around my wrists
Allowing me, on occasion, to feel her wings.
For me, the wider that I try to open my eyes, the tighter that they
Stay closed.
But I'm not blind; I'm just not ready to disturb these holy waters
Anymore than they already are. And I know that there's not a
Chance in Hell
She's ever let them be still,
Not now,   Not ever.   11-9-04

So Perfectly Smooth

How beautiful she is laying there
Feigning sleep.
The covers that were wrapped around her precious frame,
Long since abandoned her, leaving nothing
To the imagination.
Her body exposed, chilled by the morning air,
Draws me closer.
Positioned ever so carefully, she taunts me from
Every direction.
Her breasts stuffed in a bra two sizes too small,
Even her nipples have come up for air.
Her belly, so perfectly imperfect, so conveniently
Naked,
Pulls me down to her bellybutton,
Where I love to begin.
So many options when I start in the middle.
I like to go up, but I love to
Go down.
Beyond her button, lies her part that's long from
Private.
So open are her legs that even the dental floss that
She calls underwear
Can't hide the not so smooth skin underneath.
It calls to me, to my vary center,
Begging.
I don't know who wants it more, nor who will receive
The greater pleasure. 11-29-04

Down to One

After many years, I can finally see
What my marriage really is:
Broken, fragmented pieces of what it used to be.
How and when it became this way,
I don't know.
For so long I've been struggling
Lord knows, but
No matter how loud my voice gets, I'm still
Never heard.
The broken little girl with the shattered life
Created a splintered marriage and made a loving man
Bitter and cold.
I'm terrified for my children
There are many days when they are my only reason
For staying.
More than I'll ever admit.

After many years, I finally see
What my marriage really is, and yet
I stay
And let her whittle away at the
Ten percent.
That she inconsistently puts in.
I sometimes wonder what will reach
Zero
First, my patience, or her.
I'm not at zero yet, but I'm close,
And scared. 6-28-05

Regarding Everything Before (This Moment)

We've had heated days and sleepless nights,
Making big problems over little troubles.
After too many years of marriage, we both have
Our share of scars.
You show yours- to gain pity,
I hide mine-- to avoid shame.
Countless conversations we've had to try and fix
What we've broken and nothing changes because I'm
Healing on my own.
I'd be willing to accept half of the blame for
The shred of a relationship that we have left,
If only you could stop denying
Your role in the events leading up to
This moment.
After too many years,
I've finally realized that the more that we talk about
Change,
The less change happens,
And the louder I get,
The less you hear.
So, it is now, at this moment,
That I see my heart walked out
That door a long time ago and I just found the courage to
Follow it. 8-10-05

Her Mother's Daughter

Oh, to think that she would change.
What a naïve little boy I am, was
Am.
Promises are made and over-broken, to the point now
Where they're like dust blown in my face.
Love, lust and passion are like a mirage,
And my desperation for all three has gone way beyond
Thirst.
Everything that I want, I can see (in her)
At a distance
But up close everything vanishes,
I can only give out so much love before I've nothing left.
The only thing she reciprocates is anger,
Left over from a bitter childhood.
She feels that she has suffered, being the product of a broken marriage,
And now she's seeing to it that it is my turn to suffer, it's my responsibility
To pay for everybody else's mistakes.
She plans on bleeding me dry of every last bit of love until
I'm as cold as she is.
Then, when I finally leave, she will have created the very thing that she tried
To run away from. Home and marriage broken,
Herself, shattered.
This time, there will be no one there to pick up her pieces.
Everyday I wonder, will she give up, or will I give out.
There are times that I wonder if she loves me, now or ever.
Or am I simply her escape, her third and last chance at a normal life.
But she cannot be expected to learn, what she has never been taught.
Love
To her is a useless emotion that leads to more pain than pleasure, after all
She is her mother's daughter
Asleep
To her husband's heart, numb to his body.
Trying as little as she can to change,
Resulting in minute, random differences that seem to pass
With the coming dawn.
And like the stupid little virgin that I am, was
Am,
I buy it every time because I'm lonely.
I'm strangely content in my misery
Because it's mine and nobody else can take it from me.
Who would want it anyway?

9-7-05

Quiet

I'm gearing up
Weighing my options, looking at the pros
And cons. Getting ready.

I'm tired of being with a woman who is emotionally
Distant and physically unavailable.
(Or is it the other way around)?
To heal, the innocent must suffer,
And their pain will be
Unbearable to watch, but it must be
Done.
Unfortunately scars will be left.
And blame will be placed. Of course
That won't be fifty/fifty either, nothing has been yet.
I'm tired of being with a woman who doesn't know the meaning of
Compromise.
Everything is about her. Everyone else must bend or she will get
Angry.
That's the only emotion that she's ever good at.
All I want is love.
But the only time that she gets
Physical
Is when she wants something.
When we make love, it's simply to keep me
Quiet.

I'm gearing up
Weighing my options, looking at the pro's
And cons. Getting ready. 01-24-06

Misery Made Beautiful

Every night we go to bed and I
Vow that I will not touch her,
It does me no good to touch something I'll never truly
Hold.
But every night there's a piece of me that always seems to
Give in.
Ten years have passed and the same barriers
That were there the day we met, are there still today, with a few
Dents in them from years of trying
To break through them.
She seems to like her walls; although she pretends they're not
As thick or as high as they truly are.
Nothing in, nothing out, letting her stew within her own
Misery.
I'm not the one that put her there, but I am the one that is paying for it.
Everyday.
Her blind eyes see nothing wrong, and if there is something wrong, in her world
It certainly isn't her fault. 2-5-06

I

I value my ability to say how I feel even if I have to put it on paper
First.
I value my children more than anything because I finally did
Something right.
I value the
Acquaintances
That I have and hope, one day, to have
Friends
To go along with them.
I value what my marriage used to be
Not
What it has become.
I value my wife last because that's how
She makes me feel…
Last.

I value my ability to say how I feel. 02-08-06

Fallen (So Far)

I was so worried about us falling apart,
I had forgotten about me.
Eight years later, I'm beyond the help of band-aids,
I'm ignoring the fact that I'm bleeding to death.
I'll realize it when my heart is as empty as hers.
I was so worried about us falling apart,
That we broke anyway. I don't know
When or where, but we spend a lot of time walking on
Broken glass.
There are so many pieces of me missing, taken,
That I've forgotten what it is like to be me.
There is only us.
Eight years later, I don't know if I like "us" anymore.
Maybe there was never "us".
Maybe, there was only "her"
And the power she had, over "me".
I've spent so much time chasing a fantasy,
Reality never occurred as an option.
I'm too accustomed to living a lie; it's easier than facing the truth,
Sometimes.
At a time when we are supposed to be
Coming together,
Our foundation is cracking down the center.
Each is waiting for the other to jump, and yet we
Stand still.
The abyss between us is growing and we
Stand still.
I'm holding on to everything and nothing, and nothing
Will only get me so far.
After years of running in every direction at once, I have no idea
Which way to go.
I have fallen over and over again, both by her hand, and my
Crooked feet. I can't stand
To bleed any more than I already have, but what's another drop,
In the name of (the illusion of)
Love?
What's another drop, in the hope to find, what is or isn't there?
Many years have already passed, how many more will be
Sacrificed,
I'm tired of not being able to stand up, and standing tall is a hard thing to do
With her on my back all of the time. 2-25-06

Matters of the Heart

What else can I say besides I'm lonely?
How loud can I shout that I'm desperate?
How many more ways can I express my wants and needs?
Tell me before I give up, give in and walk away.
Acknowledge me for once and be true to the way you feel for the
First time in your life.
Either you love me or you don't, you were in love once or you've been a very g
Liar.
I don't know how to feel or what to believe.
There is a lack of so much in this marriage that I don't know
What is holding us together anymore.
When we finally break apart, I know somehow it will be my fault,
Matters of the heart always are. You're still learning how to use yours.
You are so beautiful, but when I look at you for too long you think
All that I want is Sex.
Your body is imperfectly perfect, and its soft touch it a rarity to my fingertips.
When I deviate from where you've allowed my hands to be, you say
All that I want is sex.
Your lips, when firm against mine, ignite a passion within my soul.
When my lips stay longer than you deem necessary, you accuse
All that I want is sex.
When we fight, if I sigh too loud or too long, look at you funny, or don't look
At you at all ,you yell
All that I want is sex.
If you would allow yourself just a moment of clarity, you would finally realize th
Sex
Is an intimate connection between two bodies, love made between two souls an
Journey of two hearts becoming one.
And right now
I'm lonely and desperate
For a connection, a love and a journey with
You.
Stop telling me go get it elsewhere, you're opening up a door that someday
I will walk through.
Whose fault is it then…Yours or mine?
All that I want I see in you.

How many more ways can I express my wants and needs?
Tell me before I give up, give in and walk away… 4-27-06

Bitter Sweet

She lives on her side of the bed these days, and I
On mine.
Back to back, cold and silent, that's how we'll
Stay.
How sweet it would be to meet in the middle
Again, but
I want it, she doesn't.
We've been on opposite sides for so long, there's no
Middle ground.
She can't fake it anymore
At least that's how it feels on my side of the bed. 8-29-06

Chasing A Shadow

I couldn't be any lonelier, even if I lived
Alone.
I'm sick of chasing a shadow, in the dark.
That's what she is.
A silhouette against my heart and I tired of not being able to feel
Her.
She's been cut up so many times by those she let get close.
All that I am left with is a string of paper dolls, reluctant to be
Holding hands, or anything else.
Pulled
At one end by her mother who bares only the title, and
At the other end, her heavenly father, who's soul concern in the
Life-after, not here not now.
He wears a cross and his collar to show his loyalty.
He has a religious shirt for everyday of the week
(And then some)
And he wears them, too thin.
We get the point.
He hides behind his religion while his daughter hides within her
Pain.
Safe within her misery.
I couldn't be any more disgusted with the mess of a
Little girl,
That these two have made, each blaming the other,
Neither,
Taking responsibility.
Mother, buys her daughter's love by giving her a credit card to use and
Abuse.
Father, swears his love to Jesus, hoping
That his back handed follow-ship to Christ will make up for the mistakes
He's made and is making with his daughter.
My wife will never tell them how she really feels.
Until she can unbury herself from all of her private pains,
She will never give me the public display of affection that I am so
Desperate for.
No random 'I love you's,'
Lasting embraces, gentle, unexpected touches.
Lingering glances, soft kisses.
No teasing, foreplay, passion,
Sex.
No love.

No love for me.
Until she learns what love is.
So I must wait or
Leave 5-22-07

One Part Hate

I hate that I have to write down my anger, when it is you that has made me this
I hate that you always bitch until you get your way, and
I hate that I give in to you.
I hate that I have sacrificed more for this marriage than you have, and
Always will.
I hate that you look so beautiful naked and you yell at me if I stare.
I hate that you turn me on and never let me get off.
I hate that I can only touch you when and where you tell me.
I hate that when we make love you always lie there with you eyes closed.
I hate that you call that making love.
I hate that you have never complimented me on my body. You make me feel ug
I hate that I compliment yours and yet you still don't want to be with me.
I hate that if we shower together you yell at me if I touch you.
I hate that when we lie next to each other you yell at me if I touch you.
All that I want is to satisfy your every physical desire and
I hate that I can't do that.
I hate that you won't do the same for me,
I hate that I have to beg to receive physical attention from you and
I hate that you don't want to do it and
I hate that I roll over and go to sleep.
I hate that you won't tell me the truth about how you feel about me.
I hate that you lie, that I caught you and yet you still deny everything.
I hate that when you look at me the way that you do, I melt.
I hate the rare occasions that you make love to me, because that's exactly what
They are, rare, and
I hate that I love it so much.
I hate that the only time you ever came after me for sex was to make a baby, no
Love, or when you wanted something from me bad enough.
I hate that you hate your parents, yet to their faces all is wonderful.
I hate that you had a terrible childhood
I hate that you knock me for not.
I hate that you love me as little as you do.
I hate that you don't know what love is. 6-5-07

Raw and Burned

I am broken, beaten, battered, bruised and scared.
I feel lonely (by now a cliché), desperate and used.
I hold on to nothing because that's all that I have left,
Though I'm not sure that I had much more when I started.
I stay because I have nowhere else to go.
And I know alone. I know isolation and desperation. After
Eight years of being married to an emotionally barren little girl who
Masquerades as a woman and a wife, I know bitterness.

I am naked, stripped of my masculinity, cut deep, bleeding and quiet about it.
I hold on to my anger because I don't know how to let go.
Neither does she.
I certainly am not here for love. Maybe once, but she never did know that word, and
Was never willing to learn it either.
I definitely am not here for sex. We don't have sex, can't make love and she doesn't
Give a fuck how physically lonely I am, or how ugly that makes me feel.

I am isolated, irritated, persecuted, tied down to a marriage that gave up on me,
Long before I gave up on it and I have the rope burns to prove it.

9-19-07

Treading Water

It's so hard to talk to Jesus when I'm married to
The Devil, and God is she beautiful.
She is the forbidden fruit on the withered tree that
Our marriage has become.
I have plenty of knowledge of Good and Evil.
I have given more than my share of silver
Just for momentary tastes of her sins.
I have denied myself countless times to keep the water still.
I pray to God to keep me strong.
Yet I am lashed and I know it.
Even still her scars lie deeper than mine.
For now
I am ignorant of the ways of other women
But I am looking
For a teacher, a lover, a friend, a companion, a partner
I want this woman to break my body the way
My wife has broken my spirit,
Baptize me in a new love;
Submerge me in her holy waters until I drown. 11-5-07

This Love

Your shattered childhood is no longer my burden.
To bear.
I'm sick of paying for your parent's mistakes, tired
Of filling a father's void to satisfy your inner child.
I need a wife. So
Look as deep as you need to, I am
No longer interested in playing a role that is not meant for me.

Your broken heart is no longer mine
To fix.
I'm sick of cutting my fingers, tired
Of being the only one willing to bleed for
This love.
Your crocodile tears no longer have any effect,
You'll get no sympathy from me. So
Talk in bitter circles all that you want, I am
No longer interested in listening.

Our splintering marriage is no longer my cross
To carry.
I'm sick of carrying all of the weight in
This union.
My legs are tired enough from dragging around my own skeletons.
It's your turn to take responsibility for a mess that you helped make,
I am no longer interested in a relationship that cannot give and receive.

My patience is wearing thin.
My anger is beginning to eclipse yours.
I've built this love, this marriage, this home, give me what's left and
Find the door. I am
No longer interested in a little girl, playing a half-ass role, to stay in a relationship that
She never wanted in the first place. 11-10-07

Back to Love

I'm trying to remember what it was like to write about
Love.
I haven't done it in a long while; I'm a little rusty
In so many ways.
After eight years together, we're in a state of dis-
Like, if you can even call it that. But
We're still together.   Barely.
Back to love,
A need that I have long since been denied.
Oh how I long for just the simplest of touches, her fingertips stroking my
Face, her fingers through my hair.
What if her lips could taste of mine for a change?

I'm trying to remember what it was like to write about
Love.
I haven't done it in a long while; I'm a little rusty
In so many ways.   1-12-08

Every Bit

I lie there, in our bed, on my side, with my back to
Every bit of her.
Silent, she brushes against me as she crosses the line between her side
Of the bed and mine
Every bit of me wants her
But nothing ever happens.
An apology maybe, for having invaded my space and then
Nothing.
She seems comfortable, wrapped tightly in these thin sheets,
Content in the isolation that we share.
I dare not say a word; she will accuse me of wanting more than I ask for.
Somewhere, deep down, I'm sure that I do.
I open my eyes as I lay there, in our bed, on my side, with my back to
Every bit of her.
Silent, in the dark, screaming for her
To touch me. 2-4-08

The 'L' Word

Let me finally commit to what I love about her.
I've spent so much time fantasizing about her that
I don't know if I can.
I fell in lust with a mirage and convinced myself that I could love her.
Strip away her anger and she really is quite beautiful. But
That armor has never quite made it to the floor. She wears it
So comfortably after nearly thirty years, though I know by now
It must be suffocatingly snug. She'll expose herself when it suits
Her purpose and then squeeze her way back in when she's done.

Let me finally admit to what I like about her.
When she's sleeping, vulnerable, and unaware that I am watching,
I wonder what she dreams, if she dreams.
I love to touch her in these brief flickering moments because
Somewhere deep within her subconscious, she gives in to my
Curious fingers and forbidden kisses, opening up, all that is safely guarded and
Locked when she is aware that other men have hurt her.
She will never admit to any physical want or need. To do that, would mean to
Surrender some of the power that she holds over me.
She'll quench my thirst when it suits
Her purpose and then she'll cast me back into the desert again.

Let me finally admit to what I loath about her. 3-18-08

Standing Still Revisited

There are many times when I feel that we've made
Giant steps in the direction we both want to go,
You've made them one way, and I, the other.
You are fighting to relive a childhood that you never experienced
The first time.
While I struggle to grow up and raise a family.
I realize now that we've only made babies, not progress.
We may not be as close as I thought (from the start)
Because I never asked you your intentions for this relationship,
I just assumed it was what you wanted.
You know what happens when you assume.
But at least *I'm* not standing still. 6-11-08

Oral Satisfaction

You don't hold me, touch me, rub me, caress me,
Kiss me, lick me suck me
Fuck me
So what do you care if I find someone else to satisfy what you won't?

You won't let me hold you, unless we are snuggling in bed
(And even then there are rules to where my hands can and cannot go.)
You won't let me touch you (there) unless you're sleeping.
The only parts of mine that are aloud to rub parts of yours are my hands
(When they are rubbing your back.)
We don't kiss anymore (nothing beyond a meaningless peck.)
Licking and sucking are the only things that I am aloud to do to you.
(You get off, I get off…I get off, you roll over and go to sleep if you are not alr
There is no making love, having sex, fucking.
So why do you complain if I'm content giving you oral satisfaction?

7-20-08

Where I Sit on Things

Sometimes
I sit here alone, with nothing
But my table lamp
Lit,
And I find comfort in the dark.
I let it hold me.
I close my eyes and let it wrap itself around me.
And yet there are other nights that I feel just how
Cold, hollow and empty it can be.
This is one of those nights, where there is no satisfaction in
Closing my eyes.
There is too much needless worry in my head tonight.
I can feel it throbbing just behind my eyes.
It's painting me pictures that I have no desire to see, and yet
They replay over and over to torment me
When I finally shut my eyes to sleep,
I barely have time to dream anymore.
I used to be full of them but now
Times are grim, money is scarce, and I don't have the time
To spend
Dreaming of things.
I've dug this grave and someday I will sleep in it.
Until then,
I sit here alone, in the dark with nothing. 12-4-08

Holding Out

It's become painfully repetitive,
What we do, in the dark.
The touching, the feeling and yet there is a lack of any
Real physical contact.
You lay there, legs open, heart closed, letting me put in
All of the work, while you shut your eyes.

After all these years it must be nice to get what I give;
The many soft, wet kisses in all of your soft wet places.
Because I still get, never
And yet,
I'm blindly, stubbornly, desperately, holding out for maybe. 1-10-09

Chapter Five: ***Nearly Over***

This chapter was the most difficult to be written. I never thought that it would actually happen and as it did, I never knew how to feel, so I felt everything all at once. The funny thing, for me, was that I could not bring myself to write as much as I thought that I would. My emotions and frustrations were at their peak and yet I couldn't focus enough to write. Maybe I tried too hard.

Two Parts Something Else

Let me take this moment,
To lay everything at your feet:
My anger, frustration, bitterness, loneliness.
I'm taking it all off, at least for now, to tell you
How I feel. To tell you
What I need, as your husband.
I need love.
Let me explain what that means to me.
It starts with the smallest of kisses or
The simplest of touches,
The dirty look in your eyes that accompanies your
Most devilish smile,
When you say 'I love you' for no reason, before
I say it to you.
The race of your fingertips through what's left
Of my hair or down my spine.
The way that you hold me when we snuggle or
When we make love in the dark.
The steady stare that pulls me in just before
We close our eyes and our lips meet.
The firmness of your lips as they kiss me back.
Your breath, soft and steady in my ear.
The way that your body reacts to mine in our
Most intimate moments.
The way that you taunt my body with yours
When you do what you do
So well.

So well.
I've bared my soul. I've expressed my needs.
I hope you can do the same. 1-25-09

In-Between This

This in-between stage is the most difficult.
We're married and yet living separate lives.
She
Comes and goes as she pleases, does nothing while
I'm trapped.
This in-between stage reveals truths that I finally can acknowledge-
She hasn't loved me for a while, and doesn't love me now,
Since declaring her want to leave.
If you ask me, she never loved me. She used me to get out of her father's house and
Raise her first child.
Now after 13 years together, she is finally old enough to stand on her own.
But I am stronger.
I think. I hope. I am.
This in-between stage is lonely.
If she stays home, we barely speak.
She'll fall asleep on the couch.
Sometimes I stare at her while she sleeps.
I close me eyes and remember what it was like to touch her is her most secret of places
I wonder if someone else is touching her there.
Lust is a very powerful sin.
I have not had an affair. Yet. I have other ways to deal. I trade
One sin for another. As many times as I need to.
I will not succumb to adultery.
Even if she has. God,
If only she were a lesbian.
This in-between stage is like walking on broken pieces of glass,
Barefoot,
Over and over again. 5-9-09

Nearly Over

I have never felt so many emotions at once.
I hate you for wanting to leave. I'm disgusted
That you waited 13 years to do it.
I love you for letting me raise the children.
I'm scared that I can't handle them.
I'm bitter that you can and will live your new life, while I
Must sacrifice even more to afford to do less.
I'm nauseous at the thought of being alone and yet
Can't stand to be in your presence.
I am defeated at the thought of 'the end' of our marriage and still
Belittled at the knowledge that it was over a long time ago,
For you.
I have felt ugly and small since you freely admitted that you have wanted
Nothing from me sexually.
Let's not forget that anytime you did get off of you back for me it was
'Just a show.'
God that burned. It still does.

Well, we've had our intermission, we're deep into the last act, the show is nearly
Let us fade to black so that I can get some relief, at least until the morning,
When everything will start to replay. 6-10-09

Comes to Shove

She pushes me away and yet I can't help but
Be drawn into her. Everyday
She moves further and further from me
And still I'm physically connected to her.
No matter how much I try to hate her, I can't.
When will I learn to let go?
The day is coming, soon, when I'll have to remove
My ring.
I don't want to.
It is the last sign that it is over .
A memory.
With nothing but a tan-line in its place. 7-5-09

In This Moment

Tonight I find a strange contentment in being
Alone.
I hold no bitterness, harbor no anger, concede no resentment.
I am simply at peace.
I have settled into a routine with my children and for the
First time I am ok
With having nobody around after they are in bed.
I enjoy the silence, for now.
It has taken many steps to get here, and I'm sure that I will
Fall backwards on occasion, so I'm just allowing myself to live
In the moment.
That's all that this might be, if I'm being truthful, simply the
Smallest of seconds.
So tonight, I look forward to a life as a single father,
Setting new goals, reaching new heights, and
Leaving her
Further behind than she left me. 7-20-09

Behind Those Guilty Eyes

We stood in the kitchen saying nothing to each other,
And I held her in my arms.
She kept her chin buried within her chest and her face hidden
Beneath her hair.
I kissed her forehead repeatedly moving down around her face until
Our lips met.
She pulled her face away from me, but not her body.
She let me put my hands down the back of her pants until I could feel
The cold skin of her beautiful ass.
I closed my eyes just to savor the moment.
I would not allow myself to become aroused for I knew this wouldn't go anywhere.
One hand then found its way up her back, tracing her spine until
It met with her shoulder blade.
I pressed her body firmly against mine, the way I would have if we were to make love.
I closed my eyes, to relish the feeling of her familiar curves.
Both hands then, claimed a breast, how I missed holding them every night as we slept.
She let me caress them, slowly, running my fingers in circles around her nipples
Until they stiffened for me one last time.
I closed my eyes, finally allowing myself to enjoy her perfectly imperfect body.
I let out a sigh of satisfaction, coupled with that of sadness.

I kissed her forehead.
She kept her chin buried within her chest and her face hidden
Beneath her hair.
Avoiding my gaze at all costs,
Until I finally let her go. 8-1-09

The Coming

Four day left until she leaves and
Doesn't come back.
Four days until I am alone.
She's begun to remove the belongings that she has deemed
Hers.
My house is broken and no amount of new furniture will fix it.
Four days until the new phase of my family begins. Just
Me and my children. How scary.
I'm afraid
That I won't be able to handle everything,
That my pocketbook won't support me,
That I'm not strong enough to raise this family
After being beat down in a failed marriage.
I can't let my children see me bleed anymore.
She's taken her fair share for the last thirteen years.

I must see this as *my* time to shine.
Four day until my resurrection.
Four days until *she's* alone.
Four days until I regain everything that she has stripped from me.
Four days until I am free.

But it doesn't feel that way.

The pain of knowing that this marriage and life, that I worked so hard to build,
Is crumbling down around my feet, drives much deeper than I thought.
It is the last scar that she will ever give me. 8-9-09

Today

So the day is here, and I, surprisingly feel
Very little.
(Other than tired.)
She came today, with her new, much older man,
(He's in his fifties with a beer gut and a mullet.)
And quietly collected her things.
I half expected myself to break down in the driveway as she was pulling away,
But I didn't.
I just kept doing what I've been doing for days,
Cleaning.
I have rearranged, thrown out, painted and scrubbed just about everything that was
Us.
I have washed her completely out of this house.
Even though I was scared to be alone, without her, right now
I am sitting proud to be on my own.
My worries now are strictly financial. Other than that I am
Strong, confident, sure of myself and my abilities as a father and positive
That my heart, now that it is mine again, can love my children more than hers
Ever could.
At least today.
Maybe everything else will hit me tomorrow when I wake up.

Did I mention he's in his fifties with a beer gut and a mullet? 8-13-09

www.ingramcontent.com/pod-product-compliance
Ingram Content Group UK Ltd.
Pitfield, Milton Keynes, MK11 3LW, UK
UKHW041922190726
13854UKWH00003B/1397

9 781257 624942